HOW TO CREATE THE WINNING MINDSET TO ACHIEVE ULTIMATE SUCCESS IN LIFE!

WIN ALL DAY

SUCCESS

Coach JC

Johnathan Conneely

WWW.COACHJC.COM

WIN ALL DAY - SUCCESS
Copyright © 2020 by Jonathan Conneely

Published by:
WIN ALL DAY Publishing
8177 S Harvard Ave.
Suite 420
Tulsa OK 74137

All rights reserved. No part of this book may be reproduced or transmitted in any form or by any means, electronic or mechanical, including photocopying, recording or by any information storage and retrieval system without written permission of the publisher except for brief quotations used in reviews, written specifically for inclusion in a newspaper or magazine.

Warning- Disclaimer

The purpose of this book is to educate and entertain. The author or publisher does not guarantee that anyone following the ideas, tips, suggestions, techniques or strategies will become successful. The author and publisher shall assume no liability or responsibility to anyone with respect to any loss or damage caused, or alleged to be caused, directly or indirectly, by the information contained in the book.

Cover and Layout Design by 1260productions.com

ISBN: 978-0-578-79927-8

Printed in the United Stated of America

A SPECIAL THANK YOU

For God

My Lord and Savior,

I would not be who I am today if it weren't for Him

For Jodi, my Beautiful Wife

My Love and Inspiration

For Mom, Dad, and my sis, Jaime

My biggest fans, Thanks for always believing in me

For My Beautiful Daughter, Alivia

I love you and am so proud of you

CONTENTS

Chapter 1: SUCCESS STARTS WITH DESIRE 20
Chapter 2: KNOW YOUR PURPOSE 23
Chapter 3: KNOWLEDGE IS POWER 25
Chapter 4: WHAT'S YOUR GAME PLAN 27
Chapter 5: TAKE ACTION 29
Chapter 6: DON'T ACCEPT FAILURE 31
Chapter 7: NO MORE EXCUSES 33
Chapter 8: LET NEGATIVITY GO 35
Chapter 9: DETERMINE YOUR ATTITUDE 37
Chapter 10: CHANGE YOUR THINKING 39
Chapter 11: DON'T FEAR FAILING 42
Chapter 12: WHAT'S YOUR PAST 46
Chapter 13: NEVER QUIT 49
Chapter 14: THINK BIG 52
Chapter 15: ARE YOU ACCOUNTABLE? 55
Chapter 16: WHAT'S YOUR SENSE OF URGENCY? 58
Chapter 17: GET BACK IN THE RACE 62
Chapter 18: EXPECT RESULTS 65
Chapter 19: WHAT YOU SOW YOU SHALL REAP 67
Chapter 20: BE A CONTROL FREAK 70
Chapter 21: HOW'S YOUR MINDSET? 74
Chapter 22: BECOME AGILE 78
Chapter 23: DETERMINE YOUR PRIORITIES 82
Chapter 24: SET YOUR GOALS 86
Chapter 25: DECIDE TO SPEAK IT 90
Chapter 26: IT'S YOUR CHOICE 95
Chapter 27: JUST DO IT 98

ABOUT JONATHAN CONNEELY

COACH JC

COACH JC IS AN ENTREPRENEUR, AUTHOR, MOTIVATIONAL SPEAKER, AND BUSINESS AND LIFE COACH.

He is the author of 4 books and has motivated audiences of all sizes through his professional speaking, including opening up for President Donald J Trump during his presidential campaign and being coined, "Trumps Hype Man".

Coach JC has empowered thousands of people to WIN in life through his books, speaking, podcasts, coaching and social media presence. He has coached and consulted professional athletes from the NFL, NBA, MLB, MLS, WNBA, and Olympians,CEO's and Pastors.

As an entrepreneur Coach JC has launched 4 companies within the personal development and business arena. He has been recognized as a 30 under 30,40 under 40,The Best of The Best, and The Young Entrepreneur of the year. Coach JC started the Non-Profit, Fit First Responders now serving over 85 first responding agencies.

Coach JC went from down and out, over $400k in debt to discover how to experience true health, wealth and happiness and now shares that message world-wide. After building his Personal Brand, using Social Media to grow his brands Coach JC became a go-to for helping other's build their Purpose Driven, Highly Profitable Personal Brand.

He is the creator and founder of the WIN ALL DAY Movement, WIN ALL DAY Academy, WIN ALL DAY Strength, WIN ALL DAY Personal Branding Academy and coaches and consults others to WIN IN LIFE.

Coach JC's greatest accomplishments are the ladies in his life, his wife Jodi, his daughter Alivia, his mom and his sister.

MEET COACH JC

Coach JC is a life coach, award winning entrepreneur, motivational speaker, and founder of the WIN ALL DAY movement.

He has been blessed to coach some of the top pro athletes, CEO's, pastors, and people from all walks of life to be their best and WIN in life. Coach JC has grown his 4 businesses through social media with over 1 million views on YouTube and over 150k followers on social media. He is the author of 4 books, the founder of the non-profit, Fit First Responders and has motivated large crowds through his professional speaking even opening up for President Donald J Trump in front of 12,000 people.

COACH JC'S STORY

From a young age, Coach JC always knew he was destined to do something big and help millions of people worldwide win in life. After throwing away his dreams, hitting rock bottom, $400k in debt, suicidal and in the fight of his life to be a father at 21 years old he went on to discover his passion and purpose in life. He created a new story and this comeback kid took what to many looked like a loss and turned it into a win. Coach JC's story will move you emotionally, inspire you to believe, empower you to change and motivate you to take action.

MAKE COACH JC A PART OF YOUR LIFE

If you would like to learn more about Coach JC and how you could partner with him to create your PURPOSE driven, PASSION filled life and HIGHLY PROFITABLE personal brand business **please visit CoachJC.com.**

A FEW WORDS OF INSPIRATION FROM THE AUTHOR

COACH JC

I love helping people create the life they were born to live! I realized through my own life and in coaching others that most people have dreams, but they have placed them on hold or have given up on those dreams for some reason. Re-awakening the dream is usually not the problem; the problem is having the RIGHT game plan and executing the essential action steps to make those dreams a reality.

> **"IF YOU WANT SOMETHING YOU'VE NEVER HAD, YOU'VE GOT TO DO SOMETHING YOU'VE NEVER DONE**
>
> **..AND DO IT EVERY DAY!"**

Success or failure is not just some big event that happens one day, but rather, it is the things or lack of things that you decide to do or not do on a daily basis.

SUCCESS IN BUSINESS OR IN LIFE IS SIMPLE...

You must first define what it is that you really want.

You must have a game plan to make that dream a reality.

You must execute the daily action steps of that gamplan.

And you must discover HOW TO CREATE THE WINNING MINDSET TO ACHIEVE ULTIMATE SUCCESS LIFE! This book will provide you with the gameplan so that you can do exactly that, CREATE THE WINNING MINDSET TO ACHIEVE ULTIMATE SUCCESS LIFE!

You can now lose that weight, have a better relationship, make more money, become a successful athlete, close more sales, and live the life that you always just wished or hoped for. How do I know? Because I did exactly that! Utilizing the same game plan that you have in this book I was able to pull myself out of a personal tragedy and create lasting success in my life.

With this same game plan, I was able to land my first job as the Director of Strength and Conditioning at the NCAA Division I level before I ever even graduated from college.

With this same game plan, I created Tulsa's first ever fitness bootcamp with no money in the bank and just eight driven women. Bootcamp Tulsa has now been named one of The Top 10 Fitness Bootcamps in the entire nation.

With this same game plan, I was able to open my dream sports performance facility, Dynamic Sports Development, and over the last 12 years have been fortunate and blessed to train some of the top athletes in the entire world.

By implementing this same game plan at the age of 29, I was named Tulsa's Young Entrepreneur of the Year, was selected as one of Oklahoma's 30 under 30 Entrepreneurs, and was also selected as one of Oklahoma's 40 under 40 Entrepreneurs.

With this same game plan I was able to build my personal brand so that I could do what I love and make a living doing it. I was able to build a national movement, "WIN ALL DAY" to help others do the same, Build Purpose Driven, Passion Filled, Highly Profitable Personal Brands.

IS THIS LUCK? HECK NO!

I tell you this because if I could do it – an Italian kid from the Jersey shore with no business or success background – then you can to!

This book is short, simple, and everything you need to know to be successful in life and in business. WIN ALL DAY - Success will not work for you unless you work it. This one book has the potential to absolutely TRANSFORM your life forever if you allow it to.

ARE YOU READY?

If so, then I have just one more question for you...

If you want something you've never had, you've got to?

DO SOMETHING YOU'VE NEVER DONE!

WIN ALL DAY

You were born a WINNER! You can WIN! You will WIN!

The only thing keeping you from getting what you really want in life is the story you keep telling yourself of why you don't have it.

To create a new story, I had to create a new belief. You don't get what you want in life, you get who you believe you are!

One of the greatest beliefs in life is a belief in YOU! Who You Were Born To Be! Who You Are! And Who You Can Become! Change your belief…Change your life!

Start to assign your life a new meaning, a new story so that you can create a new belief.

When we create a word we give it meaning and create a new way of thinking. The words we use create our reality!

WIN ALL DAY!

WIN = You were born a WINNER. You can WIN. You will WIN. You must WIN. "I am here on PURPOSE!" "I have a PURPOSE!"

ALL DAY = ALL THINGS! ALL things are possible! ALL things work together for good!

WIN ALL DAY is a BELIEF! It's a MINDSET that today is your day! "NOTHING will get in my way of me being THE BEST version of me!"

It is a DECISION. To be on a constant pursuit to walk out your calling, purpose, mission and ultimately fulfill your destiny. "I CREATE MY REALITY!"

A decision each day that "I CAN DO ALL THINGS!" To be your best, physically, mentally, emotionally, spiritually, relationally, and financially! "I AM strong!" "I AM passionate!"

A decision that no matter the situation, the circumstance, the trial and storms of life that ALL things work together for good!

"I AM FEARLESS!" "I choose FAITH!" I choose a relentless, positive, passionate, confident, intense, deliberate, joyful, encouraging, inspiring, motivating, purpose driven attitude. One of certainty, expectancy and EXCELLENCE!

Today you take on a new belief! You create a new story for your life.

And that belief is, "WIN ALL DAY!"

"I WAS BORN A WINNER!" I WILL WIN AND WIN ALL DAY" Here is your WIN ALL DAY WINNING Confession:

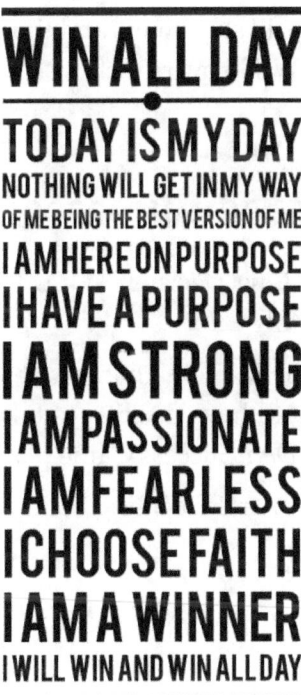

WIN ALL DAY
TODAY IS MY DAY
NOTHING WILL GET IN MY WAY
OF ME BEING THE BEST VERSION OF ME
I AM HERE ON PURPOSE
I HAVE A PURPOSE
I AM STRONG
I AM PASSIONATE
I AM FEARLESS
I CHOOSE FAITH
I AM A WINNER
I WILL WIN AND WIN ALL DAY

SEE IT. SAY IT. SEE IT.

SEE IT – See this WINNING confession at least 3x/day.

SAY IT – Say it at least 3x/day with conviction and authority.

SEE IT – Visualize yourself already there, your new belief, story, you WINNING!

WINNING IS BUILT ON WINNING

WINNING IS BUILT ON WINNING! Many people hope and wish to WIN but never WIN. Many people watch others WIN and desire to WIN but never WIN.

WINNING is built by producing small wins over and over again. I call it STACKING WINS! To build your SUCCESSFUL LIFE every day you will stack wins and those stacked wins will add up to your BIG WINS overtime!

DECIDE. COMMIT. RESOLVE.

DECIDE. What One Decision WILL I MAKE Today That Will Create Wins In My Life?

"I will make the DECISION that I want to make my greatest impact and to do that I have decided to take action and implement the WIN ALL DAY Success Game plan!"

COMMIT. What Am I Deciding Today That IS GOING TO HAPPEN in my life?

"I am deciding today to commit to be my best and create my Successful Life. To do this I am committed to executing the WIN ALL DAY Success Game plan!"

RESOLVE. What Am I Deciding Today that IS ALREADY DONE in my life?

"I am deciding that it is already done! That I will be the BEST version of me, I will create a new story for my life, I will live a life of purpose, significance and true fulfillment so that I can make my greatest impact and walk out my calling and fulfill my destiny. It is already done!"

YOUR BREAKTHROUGH IS COMING

I am not sure what motivated you to pick up this book at this time in your life but I BELIEVE that you did on purpose. There are defining moments in time when we make certain decisions that have the possibility to change it all and I believe that this moment in time will be that for you. I am not sure what your life looks like at the moment but you are making a decision to want to be more and achieve more in life and as you sow you shall reap!

As you make the decision, commit and operate with resolve by implementing the WIN ALL DAY Success Game plan, you are going to create and experience BREAKTHROUGHS in your life!

As my mentor Tony Robbins says,

"A BREAKTHROUGH IS THE MOMENT IN TIME WHEN THE IMPOSSIBLE BECOMES POSSIBLE."

Your Breakthrough Is Coming! Expect a Breakthrough in your personal and professional life as you go through this process of building your Success Life.

Personal Breakthroughs – Be expecting to create shifts in beliefs, perceptions, and standards.

Business Breakthrough – Be expecting to create strategies, ideas, systems, step by step game plans and visions to make progress in your business.

WHAT DO YOU WANT?

"Write the vision and make it plain so that you can run with it."

The Bible: Habakkuk 2:2

Before we start this journey of you building your Successful Life I want to ask you two questions...

First, What is WINNING to you? Your "What" is your VISION. If you don't know what you want you will never get it.

What does a WINNING life look like to you? What does WINNING in business look like for you?

What do you need to get out of life long term? What do you need to get from your life long term?

Where are you? Where do you want to be? Clarify the results you desire in life. A crystal clear compelling vision for the future is needed to WIN! You will define this in this gameplan and as you go through this book each day your "WHAT" will become more crystal clear and your Vision will come to life!

WHAT IS YOUR "WHY"

Second, WHY do you want to WIN? Your "WHY" is your PURPOSE. This is your driver and juice. Your motivator, the reason you do what you do! This is what pulls on you to overcome laziness, procrastination, worry, doubt, fear and to not be led by emotions and feelings.

THE GREATEST FORCE IN LIFE...
IS THE SOUL ON FIRE. A LIFE ON PURPOSE!

Why do you do what you do? Why do you have to have your "WHAT"? Think about the impact you could make? The quality of life you could have for you and your loved ones?

You have to make what's in front of you STRONGER than what's behind you!

You have to make what's inside of you BIGGER than what's outside of you!

You have to make what you want GREATER than your greatest excuse!

CREATE YOUR NEW STORY

"The only thing keeping you from getting what you really want in life is THE STORY you keep telling yourself of why you don't or can't have it!

Change your STORY. Change your life. Today is the day you stop making up stories to excuse the result you are getting at the moment.

"YOU ONLY GET A NEW RESULT BY TAKING A NEW ACTION. YOU ONLY TAKE A NEW ACTION BY CREATING A NEW STORY!"

Your story is a series of beliefs that you create around something. Change your belief, change your life! BELIEF is a feeling of certainty about what something means. The meaning of anything in life ONLY has the meaning YOU choose to give it!

What you look for, you will find! Start to assign your life, your business and anything you desire in life a new meaning, give it a new story so that you can create a new belief.

You building your Successful Life is going to be a life changing experience for you. You being able to show up on PURPOSE, with PASSIONATE and experience true success in life. But what you are really doing is creating a new story for your life.

"The true reward is the person you will become on the way to creating your new story!"

Most people never get what they want in life…or become who they were called to be because they are led by emotions and feelings. YOUR emotions no longer dictate and determine what you do. YOUR Actions do. Throughout this game plan you will take action until you act your way into feeling.

Most people want to WIN and be successful but very few people are actually running the right plays to WIN. This is your game plan, the plays you need to run to create your WINNING MINDSET and success in life so that you can create the life you desire and deserve to ultimately WIN.

"DO MY DAILY ACTIONS LINE UP WITH WHAT I SAY I WANT?"

MOTIVATION TO WIN

Motivation comes and goes. If you wait until you are motivated to take action you will never create your Successful life and WIN ALL DAY. You see, what's wrong is always available and many times we lose motivation and get stuck managing our circumstances that we don't have time to create our life!

Short term motivation comes from getting a result! Long term motivation comes from short term momentum. Using this game plan will help you to bring back the motivation by stacking wins and creating momentum. As you build your successful life you will produce these small wins each day, and over time your small wins will lead to big wins. NOW IS YOUR TIME! Let's start stacking WINS! Let's CREATE THE WINNING MINDSET TO ACHIEVE ULTIMATE SUCCESS LIFE!

CHAPTER ONE

SUCCESS STARTS WITH DESIRE

"To get what you want in life you must first make a very important choice... you must decide what it is you want!"

Coach JC

WHAT IS IT THAT YOU REALLY WANT?

If you don't know what you want you will never get it! It all starts with desire! You Must Want It! You must have a desire to achieve and a desire to succeed! So, what is that thing that you may have wished for or hoped for; that thing that you may have been dreaming about? Maybe it's to make more money, lose weight, perform at a higher level, start a business, be a great athlete, or be more successful in a certain area.

If you don't know what it is, you'll never get it! This is the big picture, the thing you dream of, your ultimate life. What does that look like to you? We all have those things that we want to get or achieve, but so many times it's just about refining it to know exactly what it is. You have to be specific about it. If you don't know where you want to go, you'll never get there. This is so important because what you desire is where your focus will go. Once you know what it is that you desire you must then place a timeline on it. When will you accomplish this desire by?

TAKE ACTION!

What is it that I really want?

How much do I really desire this?

When do I desire this by?

USE YOUR SMARTPHONE TO WATCH A MESSAGE ON HOW TO CREATE THE WINNING MINDSET TO ACHIEVE ULTIMATE SUCCESS IN LIFE!

CHAPTER TWO

KNOW YOUR PURPOSE

"Cherish your visions and your dreams as they are the blue prints of your ultimate achievements."

Napoleon Hill

WHY DO YOU WANT THAT THING THAT YOU WANT?

You have to know what it is you want and you have to determine why you want this. This is your purpose: the burning desire of why you have to have it. Your purpose is what will drive you, what is going to keep you motivated, and what is going to make your dream, your desire, become a reality. This is your burning passion to make that desire a reality. This is the reason for why you do what you do. This is the thing that you will stay focused on: the end result!

For you to truly succeed, you must know your reason why. This reason has to be specific and vivid!

TAKE ACTION!

Why do I really want this?

_____

_____

How bad do I want/need this?

_____

_____

USE YOUR SMARTPHONE TO WATCH A MESSAGE ON HOW TO CREATE THE WINNING MINDSET TO ACHIEVE ULTIMATE SUCCESS IN LIFE!

CHAPTER THREE

KNOWLEDGE IS POWER

Knowledge is like a garden: if it is not cultivated, it cannot be harvested.

African Proverb

YOU'VE HEARD IT BEFORE...

PEOPLE PERISH FOR THE LACK OF KNOWLEDGE!

I say it a little differently: "people perish for the lack of the RIGHT Knowledge!" With so much information out there it's easy to get overwhelmed and overloaded. I want you to focus now on what you really need to know to get you what you want. What do you need to do today to get the RIGHT information, to gain the RIGHT knowledge to get what you truly desire? You will always be a student and constantly be learning, but starting today, you will stay focused on the RIGHT information. Forget about everything else, my friend; knowledge is power, and today you will discover the RIGHT knowledge!

TAKE ACTION!

What knowledge do I need?

_____

_____

How will I acquire this RIGHT information?

_____

_____

By when will I have this knowledge?

_____

_____

USE YOUR SMARTPHONE TO WATCH A MESSAGE ON HOW TO CREATE THE WINNING MINDSET TO ACHIEVE ULTIMATE SUCCESS IN LIFE!

CHAPTER FOUR

WHAT'S YOUR GAME PLAN?

"I visualized where I wanted to be, what kind of player I wanted to become. I knew exactly where I wanted to go, and I focused on getting there."

Michael Jordan

DO YOU HAVE A GAME PLAN?

All successful people have a plan of action! What's yours? What's your game plan that you will execute to get you to where you need/want to be? Execute the game plan that is in your hands right now so that you can get what you desire and deserve.

Now, I want you to put together your own game plan, specific to that thing you desire. For example, if you want to be a successful athlete, what are the components necessary to become that great athlete? What are you going to do to work on your sport's skill training, strength and conditioning, nutrition, supplementation, etc.?

Today, develop your personal game plan. This should be a concrete action plan of the necessary components you will utilize to get what you want.

TAKE ACTION!

What's my Game Plan?

_____

_____

_____

_____

_____

_____

_____

_____

_____

_____

USE YOUR SMARTPHONE TO WATCH A MESSAGE ON HOW TO CREATE THE WINNING MINDSET TO ACHIEVE ULTIMATE SUCCESS IN LIFE!

CHAPTER FIVE

TAKE ACTION!

"A real decision is measured by the fact that you've taken a new action. If there's no action, you haven't truly decided."

Tony Robbins

NOW THAT YOU HAVE DEVELOPED YOUR GAME PLAN, IT'S TIME TO TAKE ACTION!

What are your daily action steps to execute your game plan? What is that one, simple, disciplined thing that you will do each and every day to get where you need to be? This is called the Law of Compounding. Time can work for you or against you. This is the step when most people fail in the road to success. Most people know what they want, but very few people's daily actions line up with what they truly desire.

This is your game plan broken up into daily action steps. This is how you are going to follow the game plan to get what it is you truly desire. You have to be very specific here. So, if you are that aspiring athlete and part of your game plan is to workout, your daily action step will be something like, "I will workout with my coach at 5:30 A.M. Monday through Friday at the gym." These action steps answer what, when, where, and how. Be as specific as possible by listing exact times, locations, and step-by step-approaches that you will take to get it done.

This written itinerary of when, where, and how you will do each daily component will transform your life forever. If you want something you've never had, you've got to do something you've never done.

TAKE ACTION!

List each area of your game plan and then list the daily action step that you will do to execute the game plan. (What, When, Where, How)

MY DAILY ACTION STEP FOR _____

IS _____

MY DAILY ACTION STEP FOR _____

IS _____

MY DAILY ACTION STEP FOR _____

IS _____

MY DAILY ACTION STEP FOR _____

IS _____

USE YOUR SMARTPHONE TO WATCH A MESSAGE ON HOW TO CREATE THE WINNING MINDSET TO ACHIEVE ULTIMATE SUCCESS IN LIFE!

CHAPTER SIX

DON'T ACCEPT FAILURE

"Success is not final, failure is not fatal: it is the courage to continue that counts."

Winston Churchill

DON'T ACCEPT FAILURE ANY MORE!

I don't care what happened in the past, and starting today, you don't care either.

Failure is not an option. Today and from here on out, you will establish the no-quit mentality, the no-quit attitude.

The only way that you will ever fail is if you don't finish. There is no other way that you can fail if you have the RIGHT game plan, your daily action steps are executed, and you stick with it!

Now get focused on the prize and Never Quit! Start today and begin to allow your vision to expand! Here is the commitment that you will use to hold yourself accountable to sticking with it.

TAKE ACTION!

My Goal(s) is(are)...

1. _____

2. _____

3. _____

"I hereby state that I will abide by my goals listed above. This commitment is between me and me. I know that I can do it! I know that I will achieve them! Failure is not an option! I will not quit until I get there. There is no stopping me! I have the discipline, the determination, and the will to achieve all of my goals! From this day forward I consider it done! I will complete my goals by _____(date)."

Signature _____
Date _____

*Hang this in a visible place where you will see it every day and say it every day.

USE YOUR SMARTPHONE TO WATCH A MESSAGE ON HOW TO CREATE THE WINNING MINDSET TO ACHIEVE ULTIMATE SUCCESS IN LIFE!

CHAPTER SEVEN

NO MORE EXCUSES

"What's more important: your excuse or what you want?"

Coach JC

YOU WILL BECOME SUCCESSFUL TODAY BY NO LONGER MAKING EXCUSES IN YOUR LIFE.

You know what they say about excuses! It's time to take responsibility for YOU! It's your body, your career, your relationship, your life! This is such a powerful thing because without it you will look at your life as a failure, keep making excuses, and never accomplish your dreams and goals. Once you take responsibility, you will begin to experience peace and joy in your life and take full control over every situation. It's time to be honest with yourself. Starting today, eliminate words like "I can't," or "but" in your vocabulary! Stop talking yourself out of getting what you truly desire. What's more important: your excuse or your desire?

TAKE ACTION!

What can I do better?

_____

_____

How can I do more?

_____

_____

USE YOUR SMARTPHONE TO WATCH A MESSAGE ON HOW TO CREATE THE WINNING MINDSET TO ACHIEVE ULTIMATE SUCCESS IN LIFE!

CHAPTER EIGHT

LET NEGATIVITY GO

"Dwelling on the negative simply contributes to its power"

Shirley MacLaine

WHAT NEGATIVE INFLUENCES IN YOUR LIFE ARE HOLDING YOU BACK FROM BEING A GREAT SUCCESS AND ACCOMPLISHING YOUR GOALS?

Starting today, it's time to eliminate negativity from your life! You know what I'm talking about! It could be someone or something that you have allowed to beat you up so badly it has kept you from what you want. You need to identify those negative things and start today to eliminate them from your life. Maybe you need to break some negative patterns or habits that you have created. These habits could include things you do, read, or watch – things that may be robbing you of your valuable time. Maybe it's someone in your life that has told you, "you can't do it," or maybe it's the environment that you are in on a daily basis that is holding you back. These negative forces in your life, both internal and external, will continue to drain you and hold you back from what you truly deserve. It all comes down to one word, my friend, CHOICE! Choose today to change the things you are doing, dissociate with negative people, change your environment, and do whatever you need to do to GET WHAT YOU DESERVE!

TAKE ACTION!

What negative things in my life have been holding me back and what will I replace them with starting today?

Negative habits? _____

    Replace with _____

Negative Individuals? _____

    Replace with _____

Negative Environment? _____

    Replace with _____

USE YOUR SMARTPHONE TO WATCH A MESSAGE ON HOW TO CREATE THE WINNING MINDSET TO ACHIEVE ULTIMATE SUCCESS IN LIFE!

CHAPTER NINE

DETERMINE YOUR ATTITUDE

"If you don't like something, change it; if you can't change it, change the way you think about it."

Mary Engelbreit

YOU'VE HEARD IT SAID, "SUCCESS STARTS WITH ATTITUDE."

I believe they almost have it right. Your attitude is the second part in the success process and crucial to your success. It all starts in your thinking and your mindset of that success. Your THINKING is what ultimate creates your ATTITUDE, your attitude creates your ACTIONS, your actions will determine your RESULTS, and your results will ultimately dictate your success and what you get out of LIFE.

So why is your attitude so important? You got it! It's because your attitude directly determines your actions! Your attitude will make the difference in how you execute the daily action steps to get to your vision. Your attitude reflects who you are, and what is on the inside is what comes out. What kind of RESULTS do you want to get? What kind of LIFE do you want to live? Your attitude is a choice and starting today you will choose to bring the attitude that lines up with getting you to your desire.

TAKE ACTION!

My attitude starting today is

_____

_____

*I choose today and each and every day to choose my attitude so that it lines up with what I desire. I will no longer allow my feelings and situations to determine my attitude for me.

USE YOUR SMARTPHONE TO WATCH A MESSAGE ON HOW TO CREATE THE WINNING MINDSET TO ACHIEVE ULTIMATE SUCCESS IN LIFE!

CHAPTER TEN

CHANGE YOUR THINKING

"Change Your Thinking, Change Your RESULTS!"

Coach JC

YOU CAN HAVE ANYTHING YOU WANT, ANY TIME YOU WANT IT, ONCE YOU CREATE THE WINNING MINDSET.

It all starts in the head, my friend. You are truly only six inches away from getting what you want. It's the six inches from your left ear to your right ear: YOUR MINDSET!

Change Your Thinking...**Change Your Life!**

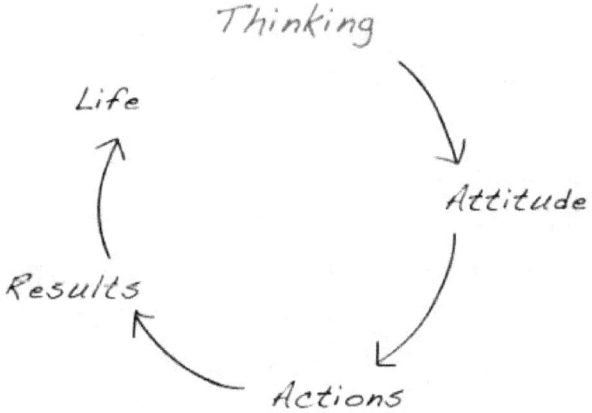

I WANT YOU TO THINK ABOUT THIS FOR A SECOND....

What is that thing you truly desire: that burning desire that you created on day one? Okay, now going off of my "Create the

Winning Mindset System" from above, I want you to envision that exact thing where it says LIFE. Check out how simple this really is.

JUST WORK YOUR WAY BACKWARDS AND ASK YOURSELF:

1. *What RESULTS do I need to get to that thing I truly desire?*
2. *What ACTIONS do I need to take to get me those results?*
3. *What ATTITUDE do I need to bring every day so my actions line up and BAM...*
4. *What am I THINKING, what's my MINDSET?!*

It all starts right there. Success or failure isn't some big event, my friend. It all comes down to how you think about it. It all starts in your head.

So many times we allow others to determine and dictate how we think about ourselves. Over time, these beliefs become a lid on our life to keep us from great success. The power of the mind is incredible! These "limiting beliefs" or "mental barriers" are real and are a lot more powerful than people believe them to be. Starting today, you must not believe what others – the media, your family members, magazines, other books, co-workers, etc. – are saying. It is time to take the lid off of your life and start to break some records. It is time to think big!

CHANGE YOUR THINKING AND YOU WILL CHANGE YOUR RESULTS!

TAKE ACTION!

What things in your thinking have been holding you back from ultimate success?

_____

_____

*Choose today to let go of this kind of thinking! Remove the negative thinking, and make a decision on a daily basis to break through your mental barriers and live the life You Were Born to Live!

USE YOUR SMARTPHONE TO WATCH A MESSAGE ON HOW TO CREATE THE WINNING MINDSET TO ACHIEVE ULTIMATE SUCCESS IN LIFE!

CHAPTER ELEVEN

DON'T FEAR FAILING

"Most of the things I have accomplished in life have been out of the fear of being mediocre."

Coach JC

THINK ABOUT IT... HOW MANY TIMES HAVE YOU PASSED UP AN OPPORTUNITY BECAUSE YOU WERE SCARED OF FAILING?

Maybe you were scared of rejection, hearing no, or perhaps, that you just may not be able to do it. Fear can keep you from relationships, career opportunities, losing weight, greater performance, and ultimate happiness and success. I've been there! Fear can paralyze you right where you're at and can become your worst enemy if you allow it to.

I want to ask you a question: What are you really afraid of? Are you scared that you won't lose the weight or maybe put it right back on? Are you scared that you may not make the sale and close the deal? Are you fearful that you may ask out the pretty woman and she may say no? Who cares?! This fear can torture you if you don't take control of it now. This fear will prevent you from achieving ultimate success. Think about how many times in your past you knew that you could have done something but did not act out of fear of failure. Really, think about it, what is the worst that could happen?

Did you know that you were only born with two fears? That's right! You were only born with the fear of falling and the fear of loud noises. This is great news for you because that means that all other fears have been created, and if you created them, then you can overcome them!

Open book test... Where does this fear of failing come from? You got it: the same place it all starts, in your THINKING! You cannot allow fear of failure to be part of your thinking, and then allow it to determine your attitude and actions on a daily basis. Instead, you will start to attack these situations in life! Overcoming fear is a two-step process.

FIRST, YOU MUST DETECT WHAT THIS FEAR IS IN YOUR LIFE, AND SECOND, YOU MUST TAKE ACTION ON IT!

TAKE ACTION!

What has fear kept me from achieving in my life?

What action am I going to take today to overcome this fear in my life?

USE YOUR SMARTPHONE TO WATCH A MESSAGE ON HOW TO CREATE THE WINNING MINDSET TO ACHIEVE ULTIMATE SUCCESS IN LIFE!

CHAPTER TWELVE

WHAT'S YOUR PAST

"You are who you are because of your past choices; who will you choose to be in the future?"

Coach JC

YOU HAVE A PAST; I HAVE A PAST; WE ALL HAVE A PAST!

Your past can be your worst enemy or your biggest ally! You can allow your past to haunt you and hold you back from great success in business and in life, or you can use it to shape you to do great things and get what you deserve.

I have seen so many people who just could not let go of the past, and they allowed their past to control their future. I don't care what happened yesterday or 20 years ago, it's done! Why allow something that is now out of your control to control you? You may have failed in a business deal, you may have not lost all the weight you desired, or you may have had a bad game... Learn from it and move on, my friend! Don't allow these feelings of depression, guilt, or anxiety control your success. If you live in the past, you will not be able to fully live in the present or in the future. Why be controlled by something you cannot currently control? Starting today, you will use your past to create future successes. I want you to think of a past situation that may be holding you back right now, and I want for you to ask yourself, what did I learn? You can take any situation, good or bad, and make it a learning experience. These past memories, good or bad, are a part of us. The key is to realize that they are not the reality of who you are right now and then use them to your advantage. So, what did you learn? Maybe something you could have done differently to get a different result, maybe put yourself into a different environment, or maybe it could have been how you reacted to the situation. What could you have done differently? What did you do wrong? What did you do right? I once heard it said, "A smart man learns from his own mistakes; a wise man learns from the mistake of others!" Learn from it and allow it to propel you to greater success.

Now is the time for you to have the success you have always hoped for. Now is the Time to Live the Life You Were Born to Live!

TAKE ACTION!

What past situation has been holding you back?

_____

What have you learned from it?

_____

USE YOUR SMARTPHONE TO WATCH A MESSAGE ON HOW TO CREATE THE WINNING MINDSET TO ACHIEVE ULTIMATE SUCCESS IN LIFE!

CHAPTER THIRTEEN

NEVER QUIT

"Quitting is losing and losing isn't winning!"

Unknown

THE ONE TYPE OF PERSON WHO HAS ALWAYS BOTHERED ME IS THE QUITTER.

I cannot stand to see someone just quit and give up! Still to this day, it angers me. This "quitter mentality" can absolutely prevent you from accomplishing what you really want in life. Over the last few years in my life coaching business, I have discovered the reason why most people give up.

Most people quit because they feel as if they don't have the ability to accomplish what they want. Well, I have GREAT news for you! Did you know that your ability is only 5% responsible for you getting what you truly desire? ONLY 5%! So what's the other 95%, you ask? For you to get the results you desire, create wealth, have a better marriage, become a professional athlete, lose 60 pounds, or close more sales, it all comes down to one word: STICKABILITY!

That's my fancy way of saying not quitting! Many people have a problem with following through until the end and giving up right before they are about to experience a giant breakthrough. Ninety-five percent of getting what you really want in life is just sticking with it, never quitting, grinding it out!

This is so important and can separate you once and for all from your competition. You need to establish a no-quit mentality – a no-quit attitude – so that you can get something you've never had. The key here comes down to the simple, small, daily action steps that you need to be taking each and every day to execute your game plan. It can't just be when you feel like it or when it's comfortable. You have to make the time and then stick with it until you get what you want!

TAKE ACTION!

What have I started that I have given up on?

_____

_____

What am I focused on right now that I will never quit at until I get it?

_____

_____

USE YOUR SMARTPHONE TO WATCH A MESSAGE ON HOW TO CREATE THE WINNING MINDSET TO ACHIEVE ULTIMATE SUCCESS IN LIFE!

CHAPTER FOURTEEN

THINK BIG

Beloved, I pray that in all respects you may prosper and be in good health, just as your soul prospers.

3 John 2

NOW IT'S TIME FOR YOU TO THINK BIG!

I have the privilege to train some of the top athletes in the world at our sports performance facility, Dynamic Sports Development, in Tulsa, Oklahoma. A lot of the athletes that we train have big dreams. It's awesome to see how big they dream: to be great in their individual sports and hopefully play at the next level. When you are doing the necessary things and executing the daily action steps, then you should expect big things. What you expect from yourself is what you will get, and what you expect from yourself is what others will expect out of you. Just like these athletes, you now have the right game plan and are executing the daily rituals so you should expect big things and big results! Don't accept being average or mediocre. Do all you do in excellence! Think Big and Act even Bigger!

You must change your thinking before you can ever change your body. You must believe you can create wealth before you ever do. You must believe you can play at the professional level as an athlete before you ever step on that field or court. You have to mentally close the sale before you ever close the sale! You have to see a great marriage with the perfect mate before you ever walk into it. Don't limit yourself by where you currently are or by what you currently have. You have so much more potential than you even believe you do, my friend! If you don't believe in yourself, why should anyone else?

When you start to Think Big and stay focused on the end result, you will find ways to make things happen so that you get what you so badly desire. Most of my clients have adopted my philosophy called, "Fake It 'Til You Make It!" I'm not talking about hoping or wishing; I'm talking about calling it now as what it WILL be!

TAKE ACTION!

*Today you will create your personal I WILL statement. This statement will be a powerful paragraph about those two or three things that you desire. You will then place this statement in three different visible areas so that each day you can remind yourself of what you WILL have. Your goal is to say this statement with authority and actually believe it each time you see it throughout the day. Be specific and vivid, and determine a specific date by which you WILL accomplish this goal.

I WILL

USE YOUR SMARTPHONE TO WATCH A MESSAGE ON HOW TO CREATE THE WINNING MINDSET TO ACHIEVE ULTIMATE SUCCESS IN LIFE!

CHAPTER FIFTEEN

ARE YOU ACCOUNTABLE?

"Accountability is making the decision to allow others to make you great!"

Coach JC

YOU WILL ONLY GO AS FAR AS YOU ARE ACCOUNTABLE!

How are you holding yourself accountable? Who are you allowing to hold you accountable? So many people get uncomfortable when they hear the word accountability. Being accountable is a great thing and a must for you to reach your goals and get what you desire! Look at almost every successful person in life and you will find that they had true accountability throughout the process in achieving that success. It will not be easy for you to get what you desire. Tough times will occur, obstacles will arise, and adversity will come at you; this is when that accountability will be able to pull you through. You have to get accountable!

There will be times when you may not feel like executing your daily actions steps. So what do you do? YOU JUST DO IT! That's right! If you want something you've never had, you can't go by how you feel, my friend! It will be nice to have that accountability in place to remind you of why you do what you do and to keep you focused on your goal.

This does not mean that I am telling you to trust everyone and anyone. What I am telling you is to find someone who you trust and respect and allow them to make you better. This is someone who wants to see you achieve your goals and live your life to the fullest. No one cares about you getting what you truly desire as much as you, but this person or people may come in a second close to seeing you succeed. This is someone who you can be totally open, honest, and vulnerable with at all times.

Accountability is simple if you're willing to be held accountable. If you think you have arrived or want to let your pride stand in the way, then this may not be that simple for you. Here's how it works: you will tell this person your goals and the game plan that you will use to get that thing you desire. Then you will fill them in on what you think is going to be the most difficult part of the process for you. This is where you will ask them to help keep you motivated and focused on the prize and not to let you quit. You will ask them to hold you accountable to your weaknesses and make sure that you are executing your daily action steps. Iron sharpens iron!

WHO ARE YOU GOING TO ALLOW TO SHARPEN YOU?

WHO ARE YOU SHARPENING?

TAKE ACTION!

How will you start today to be accountable to yourself?

Who will I contact today to allow to hold me accountable?

USE YOUR SMARTPHONE TO WATCH A MESSAGE
ON HOW TO CREATE THE WINNING MINDSET TO
ACHIEVE ULTIMATE SUCCESS IN LIFE!

CHAPTER SIXTEEN

WHAT'S YOUR SENSE OF URGENCY?

"Without a sense of urgency, desire loses its value"

John Rohn

DO YOU HAVE A SENSE OF URGENCY?

How badly do you want to lose that weight? How badly do you want to take control of your health? How badly do you want to create more wealth, have a better relationship, be a successful athlete?

Those people who make things happen in life are those that posses a sense of urgency. A sense of urgency is established when something is of great importance to you, it is a necessity. You have got to have it. A lot of times this sense of urgency can bring some pressure, but if you want to do anything worthwhile, you had better learn to appreciate a little pressure. Pressure demands that you get it done. Pressure is knowing that when you wake up in the morning you must find a way to make it happen. Pressure is lying down at night and creatively thinking of ways to make it happen. Starting today, you need to feel that accomplishing your desire is a matter of life and death.

In my own life, a lot of the things I accomplished were due to the fact that I had a sense of urgency – I had to have or needed that thing. I distinctly remember when I started to develop the attitude that I would rather be dead than live a mediocre life. It is now or never!

That is why I provide you with a WIN ALL DAY game plan. This is not just another book that you read only when it's comfortable. Get it done. Period! That is why I provide you with the exact daily action steps, so that you can stop procrastinating and get what you desire! Placing time limits on areas of your life will force you to establish that sense of urgency. You are creating this game plan to give yourself a sense of responsibility and accountability. It is also to ensure that the necessary steps are completed each day to get you to your ultimate desire.

Take action today and stay focused on the task at hand. Realize what is at the end of the tunnel. See the end result!

HOW BADLY DO YOU REALLY WANT IT?

HOW URGENT IS IT TO YOU?

TAKE ACTION!

Visualize the end result, How urgent is it to me?

_____

_____

What will I put timelines on in my life starting today?

_____

_____

USE YOUR SMARTPHONE TO WATCH A MESSAGE ON HOW TO CREATE THE WINNING MINDSET TO ACHIEVE ULTIMATE SUCCESS IN LIFE!

CHAPTER SEVENTEEN

GET BACK IN THE RACE

For a race to be finished, you must first start.

I'M A BIG FAN OF FINISHING AND NEVER QUITTING...YOU CAN'T WIN A RACE IF YOU DON'T FINISH, RIGHT?

Ask any runner and they will tell you that it's not about how you start but how you finish. That is true, but how will you ever finish if you don't start? Are you in the race? So many times in life we drop out of our race and never get the chance to see the prize at the finish line. Have you been knocked out of the race? Have you dropped out? If things don't start right, you can't just give up, you have to keep running. Maybe you have tried to get fit before, maybe you have tried diet after diet, maybe you have even hired a personal trainer, but you didn't see results, so you dropped out of the race. Maybe you were cut from the team at the first tryout so you gave up on the sport. Did you know that Michael Jordan was cut from his high school basketball team? That's right, the greatest basketball player of all time didn't even make the team and it didn't stop him. Did you know that a guy named Walt Disney was told at his first trade show that he wasn't creative enough? That's right, look at him today. Disney World is one of the world's greatest vacation destinations. So, what's your excuse? You don't have one! Today, I want you to get back into the race. Maybe this book is the starting point for your race. To finish the race, you first have to start the race. I don't care what has happened in the past, your new race begins today. Today is the day you get back into the race – the race of life. Think of every day of your life as just one lap in the competition of your race. Once that lap is over you will never get it back, and once the race is over, it's over. Life is short and once it is over it is over. There is not another race. That thing you desire is at the finish line, but how badly do you want it? Today, I want you to re-submit your name, put your sneakers on, and get back into the race. Once you get back in, then you will have a chance to win the race. You must refuse to be knocked down; you must refuse to be knocked out. Keep running, my friend, don't look back, stay focused on the end result...that finish line! This book was created to not only get you back into the race but to take you all the way to the finish line!

TAKE ACTION!

What do I need to do today to get back in the race?

What do I see at the finish line?

USE YOUR SMARTPHONE TO WATCH A MESSAGE ON HOW TO CREATE THE WINNING MINDSET TO ACHIEVE ULTIMATE SUCCESS IN LIFE!

CHAPTER EIGHTEEN

EXPECT RESULTS

"If you don't believe in yourself, why should anyone else believe in you?"

EXPECT RESULTS!

Preparation time is never wasted time, my friend, and if you are doing the things necessary to get what you desire, then you should expect results. I always tell my athletes: the ones who are disciplined and who put the time into training and preparing should expect good things. They should expect results. Once you start to implement the program and implement it to the fullest, then you should expect to see the results you desire. The mind is a powerful weapon. If you don't believe in yourself, then why should anyone else believe in you? I am not talking about being cocky and arrogant. I am talking about confidence, a confidence that you are taking care of business, that you are back in the race, and that you are not going to quit until you reach your final goal. The only one who can take you out of the game is yourself. While you are on the field you can't be defeated, while you are on the court you can't lose, while you are in the race you are the best on the track. Remember the only one who can take you out of the race is you! Start expecting results, start expecting good things, and start expecting your life to take a turn in the right direction! You can now have the peace of mind to know that you have the right program. The time of doubting yourself is over! Expect great things in your life, and expect that you will see the results you desire. Have confidence that you can do it and you will lose the weight and get fit. Expect to make more money! Expect to close more sales! Expect To Get What You Came For! Expect results knowing that you are doing what is right. Expect results now that you are taking the risks needed to take control of your life. You now have the game plan that you need to do it. You have committed to finish the race and you are focused on the end result. Now is the time to expect results; never doubt that you can do it! Start to THINK, ACT, and FEEL as if you are already there. See It, Believe It, and Expect It to come to pass.

I BELIEVE IN YOU! BELIEVE IN YOURSELF!

TAKE ACTION!

What do I expect?

_____

When do I expect this by?

_____

USE YOUR SMARTPHONE TO WATCH A MESSAGE ON HOW TO CREATE THE WINNING MINDSET TO ACHIEVE ULTIMATE SUCCESS IN LIFE!

CHAPTER NINETEEN

WHAT YOU SOW YOU SHALL REAP

"Be not deceived; God is not mocked: for whatsoever a man soweth, that shall he also reap."

Galatians 6:7

THIS IS NOT JUST SOME SPIRITUAL SAYING FROM THE BIBLE BUT A UNIVERSAL LAW IN LIFE.

I have found it to be very true in many different aspects of life. "What you sow, you will reap." If you sow badly, you will reap badly; if you sow well, you will reap well. If all you eat is junk food, you will reap the negative effects of that junk food. If you sow the time to close more sales you will close more sales. If you want to have a better relationship, invest the time to sow good seed into that relationship. As you start to follow the game plan, you will reap the benefits of being one step closer each day to your goal.

How much time are you sowing into getting what you want? How much effort are you sowing into your daily action step to get what you desire?

It's not just about doing it but doing it the right way. You've probably heard it said: practice makes perfect. Not necessarily! Practice makes permanent. Practicing the right way makes perfect. Perfect practice makes perfect! Are you sowing the right seed? Are you practicing the RIGHT way? Stop wasting your time staying busy and start investing your time wisely by being productive! Start today to make sure that you are sowing the RIGHT seed on a daily basis to get you to reap the ultimate reward.

IF YOU WANT SOMETHING YOU'VE NEVER HAD,

YOU'VE GOT TO DO SOMETHING YOU'VE NEVER DONE!

TAKE ACTION!

Am I sowing good seed on a daily basis to get what I desire?

_____

_____

What can I do better or more of to reap what I desire?

_____

_____

What am I going to do that I've never done so that I can get what I've never had?

_____

_____

USE YOUR SMARTPHONE TO WATCH A MESSAGE ON HOW TO CREATE THE WINNING MINDSET TO ACHIEVE ULTIMATE SUCCESS IN LIFE!

CHAPTER TWENTY

BE A CONTROL FREAK

"First we make our habits; then our habits make us."

Charles C. Noble

YOUR FUTURE IS IN YOUR HANDS.

You control your future, and you determine what happens now, tomorrow, and forever. You are where you are today because of the decisions you made yesterday. You will be who you are in the future based on the decisions you make today. I talk to so many people who have allowed other people and other people's situations determine where they are currently. It's time you take responsibility for your actions. No one forces you to do what you do and no one forces you not to do it. You are in complete control of your life, and now by lining up your daily rituals you can change your life forever.

Many people let their bodies get so out of shape and don't want to take control of the outcome. No one made you eat McDonald's every day! You are at this point in your life today because of the choices that you made yesterday. You control your future, and you control your life.

BE A CONTROL FREAK. IT'S YOUR LIFE! TAKE CONTROL OF IT!

This is why your desire must be strong; it must be strong enough to overcome mental laziness. Some people want the easy way out because they have allowed their mental laziness to create an attitude of laziness, which has produced daily laziness in their actions. NOT YOU! Do not allow mental laziness to determine your future. I won't let you do it. Not any more! You have to make a choice to no longer blame others for where you are at in life and to no longer complain about what you don't have. You must make the choice to overcome mental laziness. You control it, my friend! Stop settling because it's comfortable or easy at the moment.

> **ARE YOU SACRIFICING WHAT YOU WANT MOST IN LIFE FOR WHAT YOU WANT AT THE MOMENT?**

You know what you want! Is what you want at the moment more important than getting what you want most in life? Do you want that 30-pound weight loss or that brownie more? Do you want to make that $50,000 extra a year or watch that movie? Do you want that professional contract or that late night at the club?

IT'S YOUR CHOICE, YOU CONTROL THE OUTCOME

TAKE ACTION!

What areas of my life have I been allowing others to control?

What do I want most in life?

USE YOUR SMARTPHONE TO WATCH A MESSAGE ON HOW TO CREATE THE WINNING MINDSET TO ACHIEVE ULTIMATE SUCCESS IN LIFE!

CHAPTER TWENTY ONE

HOW'S YOUR MINDSET?

"You can have anything you want, any time you want it, once you change your thinking!"

Coach JC

IT WAS MAY 6, 1954, AND NO RUNNER COMPETING IN TRACK AND FIELD HAD EVER RUN A MILE IN LESS THAN FOUR MINUTES. All the so-called experts and commentators declared that it would never be done. Studies were performed to show that it was not humanly possible and that no one could possibly run that fast for that long in order to make it happen. For years those tests and studies stood true, and no one broke the four-minute mile barrier. However, on that day in 1954, a man named Roger Bannister made sports history and ran a mile in 3 minutes and 59 seconds! Up until that point, the runners had allowed the opinions of others to dictate their outcome. Roger Bannister trained hard and did not believe what all the experts were saying. He did not believe that it was impossible. He refused to let others determine his outcome, and he believed that he would break that four-minute mile run. He did not allow others to put a limit on his life. He was going to determine his own future and his own destiny.

This story is so fascinating not only because Roger Bannister made history but also because of what I am about to tell you: just 46 days later, another runner broke his record. Now, after more than 50 years, hundreds of runners have run a mile in less than four minutes! I want you to think about that. For hundreds of years no one could run the mile in less than four minutes. It was pretty much accepted that no man could break the four-minute mile barrier. It was believed that the four-minute mile was physically impossible. It was commonly accepted as a fact! However, the reality was that the four-minute mile was a psychological barrier!

SO WHAT HAPPENED? I WILL TELL YOU.

For all those years, athletes allowed others to set that barrier in their minds. For all those years runners believed what others said. Everyone was convinced that it was impossible. The lid was put on their abilities. The power of the mind is incredible! These "limiting beliefs" or "mental barriers" are real and are a lot more powerful than people believe them to be.

I am here to tell you that you can't believe what others are saying: the media, your family members, magazines, other books, co-workers, etc. It is time to start to break some records. It is time to think big! Change your thinking and you will change your results.

IT'S TIME TO THROW THE LIDS OFF OF YOUR LIFE!

TAKE ACTION!

What is your four-minute mile barrier?

_____

_____

What things in your thinking have been holding you back from ultimate success?

_____

_____

CHOOSE TODAY TO LET GO OF THIS KIND OF THINKING!

USE YOUR SMARTPHONE TO WATCH A MESSAGE ON HOW TO CREATE THE WINNING MINDSET TO ACHIEVE ULTIMATE SUCCESS IN LIFE!

CHAPTER TWENTY TWO

BECOME AGILE

"Don't let obstacles stop you. If you run into a wall, don't turn around and give up, figure out how to climb it, go through it, or work your way around it."

ARE YOU READY? YOU HAD BETTER BE!

Obstacles are going to occur, times are going to get tough, the road will be rocky, adversity will arise, and uncomfortable times will happen. This is a guarantee, my friend. The question is not, will it ever happen? Instead, the question is: what are you going to do when these inevitable circumstances occur? Starting today, you need to become agile. Being agile is a huge component of being a great athlete. We train our athletes to become more agile so that they can perform at the highest level. Hindrances are going to come; that's why the key is preparing for them now. How will you react?

Circumstances happen, both good and bad. Some you can control, and others you just can't control. The name of the game is to prepare how you will react to these circumstances when they come. How you react will determine the outcome.

Agility is defined as the ability to get from point A to point B in the shortest amount of time, while losing the least amount of motion. For you to be successful and to accomplish what you desire, you will need to become agile both physically and mentally. When your mind becomes agile, you will be able to conquer anything. Watch how quickly the pounds fall off! Watch the wealth you start to create, the success you start to experience and the life you start to live. What are you going to do when obstacles come at you? You have to do whatever it takes to not let them stop you. Nothing can stop you! I don't care if you have to go through, around, over, or under. Whatever you have to do you must do it. This is something that is developed; increasing your mental agility can be trained just like physical agility in an athlete. You must make a conscientious effort on a daily basis to fight through obstacles and not react based on how you feel but rather in the way that will get you the outcome you desire. Every day a situation will arise that will make you uncomfortable, so practice becoming more agile. Use daily circumstances to make yourself better so that when the large obstacles are thrown at you, you will know how to react.

STARTING TODAY I WANT YOU TO LEARN HOW TO BECOME COMFORTABLE BECOMING UNCOMFORTABLE.

TAKE ACTION!

How will I choose to react to a certain situation that will get me the outcome I desire?

How will I become comfortable today becoming uncomfortable?

USE YOUR SMARTPHONE TO WATCH A MESSAGE ON HOW TO CREATE THE WINNING MINDSET TO ACHIEVE ULTIMATE SUCCESS IN LIFE!

CHAPTER TWENTY THREE

DETERMINE YOUR PRIORITIES

"You can always tell what someone really wants in life by looking at their priorities."

WHAT ARE YOUR PRIORITIES?

Do you know why a lot of people are overweight and never lose pounds? Do you know why so many people wish to make money and never make it? Why so many kids dream of being a professional athlete but never achieve it? It's simple... It's because doing the daily action steps to get them to their goal was never made a priority. What is it that you really value in life? You can always tell a person's desires and values by their priorities. What are your priorities?

Now is the time to address the priorities in your life! I'm not talking about what you may say your priorities are but rather what your actions really reflect. Your priorities are not expressed by what you say; instead they are determined by your daily actions. You may know in your heart that you want to lose weight, make more money, have a better job, create better relationships, but that doesn't matter... it's the follow through, the action, that is slowing down your progress. Starting today, you will need to make sure that what you ultimately want becomes a priority in your daily actions steps.

TAKE ACTION!

COACH JC'S FIVE STEPS TO PRIORITIZE YOUR PRIORITIES:

1. *Know what you want – don't waiver from it. What Do I want?*

   _____

   _____

2. *Write it out – Make it clear and be specific and realistic. What are my Top 5 Priorities in getting what I want?*

   _____

   _____

3. *Live it out – Walk it out on a daily basis. Be who you say you are! Who am I?*

   _____

   _____

4. *Associate Yourself – Surround yourself with people who have similar priorities. Who will I surround myself with?*

----

5. *Give it a check-up – Re-evaluate your priority list on a weekly or monthly basis. When will my scheduled check-up be each week/month?*

NOW, STOP TALKING ABOUT IT AND GO AND GET IT!

USE YOUR SMARTPHONE TO WATCH A MESSAGE ON HOW TO CREATE THE WINNING MINDSET TO ACHIEVE ULTIMATE SUCCESS IN LIFE!

CHAPTER TWENTY FOUR

SET YOUR GOALS

"Setting goals is the first step in turning the invisible into the visible."

Anthony Robbins

IF YOU DON'T KNOW WHAT YOU WANT, YOU WILL NEVER GET IT.

If you don't know where you are going, you will never get there. Setting goals will help lead you to where you want to go in life. That's what this whole book is about: discovering what you want and taking the necessary daily action to go and get it! Knowing where you want to go will enable you to concentrate your daily activities, actions, and efforts on the things that are necessary to get there.

I am never amazed when I sit down with a client and I ask them, "What are your goals?" They may say to play in the NBA, to lose 35 pounds, to pack on 25 pounds of muscle, to buy a new home, to make more money. Most people don't even need to think about it. A lot of people have determined their ultimate long-term goal, and that is great. I then follow up by asking them, "What are you doing to get there?" Very few people set short-term goals. How much money do you want to make in the next 90 days, how many sales do you need to close in the next 30 days, how much weight will you lose this month? These short-term goals are the small rewards leading to the big prize at the end. Once you have determined these short-term goals, the question is: what do you need to do on a daily basis? What about on a weekly basis? Or even a monthly and annual basis to get to this ultimate goal? Goal setting is crucial, but without the game plan to get you there, you will never complete those goals.

IN THIS BOOK, STARTING TODAY, YOU ARE GOING TO SET GOALS ...AND HAVE FUN DOING IT.

TAKE ACTION!

My Ultimate Goal is,

_____,

and I will accomplish this by _____ *(date)*

My 1-year Goal is

_____,

and I will accomplish this by _____ *(date)*

My 30-day Goal is

_____.

USE YOUR SMARTPHONE TO WATCH A MESSAGE ON HOW TO CREATE THE WINNING MINDSET TO ACHIEVE ULTIMATE SUCCESS IN LIFE!

CHAPTER TWENTY FIVE
DECIDE TO SPEAK IT

"All our dreams can come true if we have the courage to pursue them"

-Walt Disney

THIS IS ALWAYS A DIFFICULT STEP FOR PEOPLE TO DO.

I want you to begin to speak those things that you desire and want to accomplish in life. Let me start by saying that I don't believe you can just repeatedly say that you want something and it will happen. I am talking about speaking with a confidence and a positive attitude, while at the same time believing without a doubt that those things that you are taking action on will come to pass. If you repeatedly say, "I am going to lose those 20 pounds!" Then you will subconsciously find ways to make yourself lose those 20 pounds. You will start to believe that it is already a reality; therefore, you'll do what's necessary to make it happen. There is tremendous power in your words, my friend. This can work against you also if you allow it to. If you keep saying, "I'll never lose these 20 pounds," you won't make any effort, and you will eventually quit because your subconscious mind will have accepted that you will never lose the weight.

The other reason I believe that this is so powerful is that you will have people who will speak against you accomplishing your goal, people who do not want you to succeed, and people who will doubt that you can do it. The way to counteract this negativity is for you to defeat them by speaking what you desire into existence. When you speak against this negativity, you are releasing your confidence, and you are exposing yourself to positive energy. You will never really experience true success in your life if you are negative and are always speaking depressing and doubtful things. When you constantly speak negatively, it will make you unpleasant to be around and very unhappy. Who wants to be around those kinds of people? I am a big action guy, and you should feel confident to do this because you are putting action behind the words! Here is the cool thing: speaking your goal into existence can considerably improve your results and how you feel about yourself and others.

It goes back to the premise that what you sow is what you will reap. Now, why is this so powerful for you? It is because you are not only speaking it, but you are putting action behind it while you speak it. Here's what I mean: I want you to not just speak it, but SPEAK IT WITH AUTHORITY. Say it like you mean it. Use the tones and pitches in your voice; use the nonverbal communication of your body language to express what you really want. Speak it with visualization and imagination and start to see that very thing that you are speaking! That is what the game plan is all about, and that is a powerful combination!

It always makes me laugh when someone says that there is no power in words. Think about it for a second... Think about something someone said to you as a kid that was hurtful. Chances are you can probably recall something that was said. You have never forgotten it! In fact, it may even still bother you. Maybe someone told you that you couldn't do something, and then you started to think that maybe you couldn't, and it stopped you from accomplishing something in your life. On the flip side, has anyone ever said something so positive to you that it encouraged you to take a step in your life that you were afraid to take? I know that this has happened to me.

THERE'S POWER IN YOUR WORDS!

TAKE ACTION!

Create your 'I am' Statement today and start to say it each day with Authority, with Visualization, with Imagination! Your 'I am' Statement

_____

_____

_____

_____

_____

USE YOUR SMARTPHONE TO WATCH A MESSAGE ON HOW TO CREATE THE WINNING MINDSET TO ACHIEVE ULTIMATE SUCCESS IN LIFE!

CHAPTER TWENTY SIX

IT'S YOUR CHOICE

"Are you going to sacrifice what you want most in life for what you want at the moment?

-*Unknown*

HOW BADLY DO YOU REALLY WANT IT?

How badly do you really want to have success in life? How badly do you really want to make more money? How badly do you really want to have that great marriage or job? Well, I have great news for you. Now you can; Now is your time! You may be saying to yourself, "It is just not that simple coach." Of course it is. All it takes is one choice. Just one decision – made by you! As you probably realize, much of life is a routine, and I have seen a lot of people become stale and stagnant. If you are not careful, it is very easy to fall into this trap. Make a decision starting today that you are not going to live another day on cruise control. Make a decision today that you are not going to allow your life to become stagnant. Have some passion about who you are, and make the decision to be passionate about what you are doing. It's your choice! Yes, it is that simple. So many people allow others to make decisions for them on a daily basis; they allow people to choose their future for them. Not me and not you! You may not have the perfect body, you may not have the perfect job, you may not live in the perfect environment, but remember, you can still choose to change any of that. It is just a choice, just one decision! Today, you are choosing to take control of your life by taking control of your THINKING. Today, you are choosing to take control of your life by taking control of your ATTITUDE. You choose your ACTIONS. You choose your RESULTS. You choose what your life looks like. You choose how much money you make. You choose what religion you practice. You choose what kind of marriage you have. You choose just about everything that happens on a daily basis. You choose who you are. It's YOUR choice!

STARTING TODAY, I WANT YOU TO MAKE A DECISION.

Make the decision that your life is valuable and that you are worth it. You are done thinking about it! Starting today, you will no longer make excuses, and you will no longer accept anything else but greatness. You will no longer accept anything but results! Start to make some big choices that are going to lead to big results. You must make a decision, a choice, to create an opportunity in your life that you may not have had otherwise.

TAKE ACTION!

What choice will I make today that will take me closer to my goal?

_____

_____

_____

_____

_____

USE YOUR SMARTPHONE TO WATCH A MESSAGE ON HOW TO CREATE THE WINNING MINDSET TO ACHIEVE ULTIMATE SUCCESS IN LIFE!

CHAPTER TWENTY SEVEN

JUST DO IT

> *"Do it, and then you will feel motivated to do it."*
>
> Zig Ziglar

NOW IT IS YOUR TIME!

You have learned over the last 26 chapters how to create the WINNING MINDSET, take massive action each day, and have anything you want any time you want it.

This chapter's short and sweet, my friend. You have everything you need to be successful. There is just one more thing left... JUST DO IT! Like our friends at Nike say, JUST DO IT!

It's simple. It really is... if you just do it! All you need to do is stay focused on the end result and do your one, simple, disciplined thing each day.

I want for you now to commit to not just doing it, but to doing it in the best way that you possibly can. No more average! No more mediocre! So many people do things half-heartedly and just cruise through life. I am telling you that what you put into it is what you will get out it. It goes back to how badly do you want this? I want you to really think about this: in just 27 days, your life can be different! In just 27 days, you could be on your way to ultimate success! In just 27 days, you can have the body you have always desired! In just 27 days you can create more wealth! IN JUST 27 DAYS, my friend! Can you give it everything that you've got? Can you not just do it, but do it like there is no tomorrow? Is your life worth it?

ACTIONS SPEAK LOUDER THAN WORDS: SHOW ME WHAT YOU'VE GOT! JUST DO IT!!!

TAKE ACTION!

Today I want you to go back to page one and start to refine all your daily actions steps for the next 27 days. Know Your Desire, Know Your Game Plan, and Know Your Daily Action Steps that will take you there.

USE YOUR SMARTPHONE TO WATCH A MESSAGE ON HOW TO CREATE THE WINNING MINDSET TO ACHIEVE ULTIMATE SUCCESS IN LIFE!

CONGRATULATIONS!

You did it! You completed *WIN ALL DAY - Success* game plan so that you can ACHIEVE ULTIMATE SUCCESS IN LIFE!

The principles that you have just read are simple, and they work if you just work them. Once you transform your thinking, you will be able to have that thing or things that you so badly desire.

THE CHOICE IS YOURS, MY FRIEND!

Remember, success is not some big event that just happens. It comes down to you executing your daily action steps and exercising the law of compound in your life. No one else can do it for you. Time can work for you or against you! What's your choice? How badly do you want this success?

I believe in you and know that you desperately want it. Listen to me, don't get overwhelmed, just follow the game plan and execute that one simple, disciplined thing every day that will get you to the promise land!

SO, WHERE DO YOU GO FROM HERE?

YOU WIN, AND WIN ALL DAY!

1. Create and Stack WINS. You have created your game plan so now it is your time to live it out. Starting today, start to STACK WINS.

2. The Next Level. Now that you have Created The WINNING MINDSET it is time to take it to the next level. What is next for you? What goals, dreams and ambitions do you have in life?

3. Make It Happen. Go and get it! Make your dreams a reality.

4. Get a Coach. ALL successful teams have coaches. Leaders are led by other leaders. You want to WIN, get a coach. A coach can fast track your results and save you alot of time and money on your road to WIN.

5. Apply To Work With Us. On the next few pages you will see a few way to work with us. Through our WIN ALL DAY Academy you can live the life you were born to live!

YOU WERE BORN A WINNER!
WIN ALL DAY!

Coach JC

CREATE YOUR PURPOSE FILLED, HIGHLY PROFITABLE PERSONAL BRAND!

PURPOSE | PASSION | PROFIT

With over 54 step by step lessons, Action Guides, and over 23 hours of Coach JC personally coaching you every step of the way, together we will create your passion filled, purpose driven, highly profitable personal brand, so that you can do what you love, make your greatest impact and make money doing it!

WINALLDAYPERSONALBRAND.COM

TRANSFORM YOUR BODY. TRANSFORM YOUR LIFE. IN ONLY 6 WEEKS!

FOCUS | FITNESS | FOOD | FAMILY | FAITH

Lose Weight, Get Fit & Build Strength with Online Workouts, Nutrition & Accountability. ANYTIME. ANYWHERE.

WINALLDAYSTRENGTH.COM

Learn how to :

- Create your purpose driven, highly profitable brand.
- Create the winning mindset to achieve ulitmate success in life.
- Look, feel and perform your best with a 27 day gameplan.
- Create the winning mindset to win as an athlete and win in life.

GET YOURS TODAY AT WWW.COACHJC.COM

REQUEST COACH JC FOR YOUR EVENT

Jonathan Conneely, Coach JC, is available for speaking engagements at conferences, departments and agencies.

ORGANIZATIONS BRING IN COACH JC TO SPEAK ON THE TOPICS OF:

Leadership | Teamwork
Motivation | Culture Development
Mental Conditioning | Personal Branding

TO MAKE COACH JC A PART OF YOUR NEXT EVENT PLEASE CONTACT US:

1-800-382-1506
email: info@coachjc.com

www.CoachJC.com

www.ingramcontent.com/pod-product-compliance
Lightning Source LLC
Chambersburg PA
CBHW051455290426
44109CB00016B/1767